THIS BOOK BELON

NAME:
_____

GRADE:
_____

TEACHER:
_____

SCHOOL:
_____

G.L.A.T. Mathematics Practice Test Workbook Grade 6

Authored by Bahamian Teachers United

Published by BSM Consulting

Copyright © 2020/2021

All Rights Reserved.

No part of this publication may be reproduced or distributed in any form or by any means, or stored in a database or retrieval system, without the prior written consent of BSM Consulting, including, but not limited to, network storage or transmission.

ISBN: 978-1519743459

DISCLAIMER: This book has been adapted from the G.L.A.T. Mathematics Papers for Grade 6. The questions have each been modified slightly in adherence to the copyright laws of The Commonwealth of The Bahamas.

TABLE OF CONTENTS

MATHEMATICAL CONCEPTS
- MATHEMATICAL CONCEPTS – MAY 2011 4
- MATHEMATICAL CONCEPTS – MAY 2012 13
- MATHEMATICAL CONCEPTS – MAY 2013 20
- MATHEMATICAL CONCEPTS – MAY 2014 26
- MATHEMATICAL CONCEPTS – MAY 2015 32
- MATHEMATICAL CONCEPTS – MAY 2016 37
- MATHEMATICAL CONCEPTS – MAY 2017 43
- MATHEMATICAL CONCEPTS – MAY 2018 48
- MATHEMATICAL CONCEPTS – MAY 2019 55

COMPUTATION
- COMPUTATION – MAY 2011 61
- COMPUTATION – MAY 2012 65
- COMPUTATION – MAY 2013 68
- COMPUTATION – MAY 2014 70
- COMPUTATION – MAY 2015 72
- COMPUTATION – MAY 2016 74
- COMPUTATION – MAY 2017 77
- COMPUTATION – MAY 2018 80
- COMPUTATION – MAY 2019 83

APPLICATION
- APPLICATION – MAY 2011 87
- APPLICATION – MAY 2012 96
- APPLICATION – MAY 2013 105
- APPLICATION – MAY 2014 114
- APPLICATION – MAY 2015 124
- APPLICATION – MAY 2016 132
- APPLICATION – MAY 2017 141
- APPLICATION – MAY 2018 147
- APPLICATION - MAY 2019 156
- REFERENCES 164

MATHEMATICAL CONCEPTS – MAY 2011

1. Write the number 7 143 524 in expanded form.

   Answer:_____
   _____[1]

2. Write the number that is needed in order to complete the sequence.

   | 59 743 | 59 748 | |

   Answer: _____[1]

3. What place value has the number shown been rounded to?

   4,293,540 to 4,300,000

   Answer: _____[1]

4. From the given number write down the following:

258 539.614

(a) The name of the digit in the thousandths place.

Answer: _____[1]

(b) The value of the digit 3 in the number.

Answer: _____[1]

5. Write the number that is represented by the Roman numeral.

MCMXCV

Answer: _____[2]

6. Re-write the date below using the Systems International format.

> **October 12th, 1492**

Answer: _____[1]

7. Which **TWO** properties of addition are shown in the equation?

> **36 + 2 = 2 + 36**

Answer: (i) _____[1]

(ii) _____[1]

8. Express $6\frac{2}{5}$ as an improper fraction.

Answer: _____[1]

9. Use the chart to answer question 9 (a) and (b).

	FRACTIONS	DECIMALS	PERCENTS
(a)	$\frac{1}{5}$	0.20	
(b)	$\frac{12}{20}$		60%

(a) Write the percent that will complete question (a).

Answer: _____[1]

(b) Write the decimal that will complete question (b).

Answer: _____[1]

10. (a) Draw the pattern of dots to show the triangular number array for 45

[2]

(b) If the triangular number array from question 10(a) is continued, what would the next number in the sequence be?

Answer: _____ [1]

11. Write the name of the types of lines shown in the below diagram.

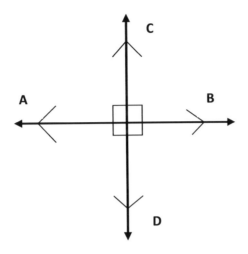

Answer: _____[1]

12. Use the below diagram to answer questions 12 (a) and (b).

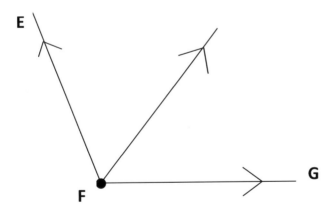

(a) Name the type of angle that is formed by EFG.

Answer: _____[1]

(b) What is the name of the point that is represented by F?

Answer: _____[1]

13.(a) Circle the shape inside the box that shows an irregular polygon.

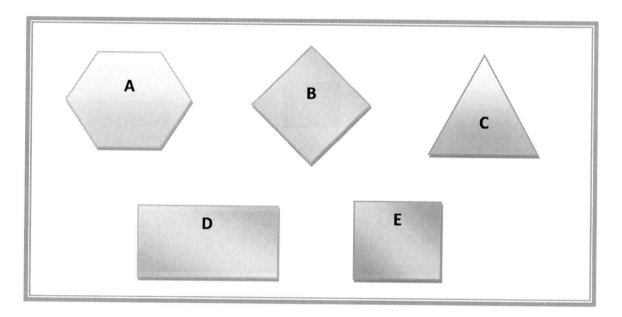

(b) Name each shape:

    A: _____[1]

    B: _____[1]

    C: _____[1]

    D: _____[1]

    E: _____[1]

14. Look at the solid figure. Name two plane figures that have been joined together to make up the solid figure.

Answer: _____[1]

_____[1]

15. Use the diagram below to answer questions 15(a) and (b).

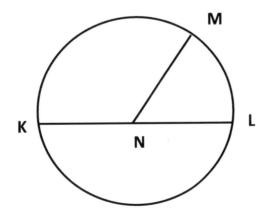

(a) Write the name of the line labeled 'MN'

Answer: _____[1]

(b) The line labeled 'KL' can be called by two names. List the two names.

(i) _____[1]
(ii) _____[1]

MATHEMATICAL CONCEPTS – MAY 2012

1. Using the digits 2,0,9,1 arrange them to make the smallest decimal number possible.

   Answer: _____[1]

2. Write the dollar amount shown on the cheque in words.

Jennifer Hendricks	0010
People's Bank of the Bahamas	October 23rd, 2014
Pay to the order of **Nassau Electrical Company**	$12,105.47
_____ dollars	
Memo: Electrical Bill	N Major

   Answer:
   _____
   _____ [1]

Use the picture to answer question 3 (a) & (b).

3. (a) Write the square number that is represented by the array.

   Answer: _____ [1]

   (b) Write the equal factors for the square number from (a).

   Answer: _____ [1]

4. Continue the pattern then write the next number in the oblong number pattern to complete it.

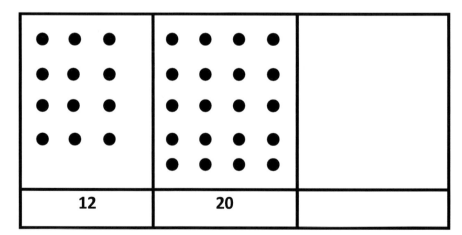

5. Place the symbol < or > in the shape to compare the groups of numbers.

   (a) **73 586** ◯ **73 168**

   (b) **73 274** ◯ **73 608**

6. Write the inverse operation for **325 ÷ 5 = 65**

   Answer: _____ [1]

Use the picture to answer question 7.

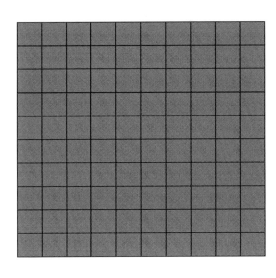 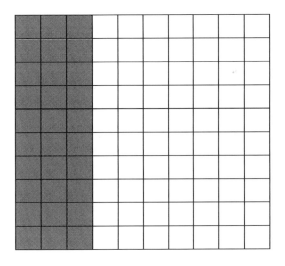

7. (a) Write the fraction that the picture represents.

   Answer: _____ [1]

   (b) Write the decimal that the picture shows.

   Answer: _____ [1]

8. Fill in the missing fraction to complete the number sentence.

$$\frac{6}{8} + \underline{} = \frac{7}{8}$$

Answer: _____ [1]

9. Express $\frac{63}{5}$ as a mixed fraction.

Answer: _____ [1]

10. Place an "X" on the diagrams that represents a pair of equivalent fractions.

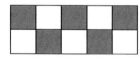

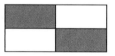

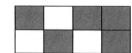

[1]

Use the pictures to answer question 11 (a) & (b).

11. Write a ratio which shows the following:

(a) Conch shells to starfish

Answer: _____ [1]

(b) Conch shells to both conch shells and starfish.

Answer: _____ [1]

12. Write the end time to complete the chart.

START TIME	ELAPSED TIME	END TIME
6:55 p.m.	45 minutes	?

Answer: _____ [1]

Use the street map to answer question 13 (a) and (b).

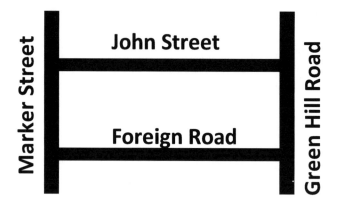

13. State the mathematical name for the type of line that is represented by the directional flow of the following:

(a) Green Hill Road and Marker Street

Answer:_____ [1]

(b) Green Hill Road and Foreign Road

Answer: _____ [1]

Use the image below to answer question 14 (a) and (b).

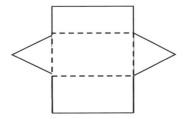

14. (a) Name the solid figure that would be formed when the faces of the net shown are connected.

Answer: _____[1]

(b) Complete the table to describe the solid figure formed from the net in 'a'.

SOLID FIGURE	NUMBER OF FACES	NUMBER OF EDGES	NUMBER OF VERTICES

[3]

15. Choose the best term from the box to complete each statement.

Composite Number   Multiple   Prime Number   Factor

(a) A number that has exactly two factors _____ [1]

(b) A number multiplied by another number to find a product

_____ [1]

For Answer Key Go To:

http://greatminds.teachable.com/courses/glat-workbook-answer-keys/

MATHEMATICAL CONCEPTS – MAY 2013

1. Write 7 832 940 065 in expanded form.

   Answer: _____
   _____ [1]

2. Write thirty-five and two hundred nine thousandths in

   (a) Standard form

   Answer: _____ [1]

   (b) Expanded form

   Answer: _____ [1]

3. (a) Round 96 374 to the nearest ten

   Answer: _____ [1]

   (b) Round 96 374 to the nearest ten thousand

   Answer: _____ [1]

20

4. Using the number 637.2

   (a) Increase it by 1000. Write the new number.

   Answer: _____ [1]

   (b) Decrease the answer by 500. Write the new number.

   Answer: _____ [1]

5. Using the number '10' as a base:

(a) Write 1000 in exponent form.

Answer: _____ [1]

(b) Write 1000 as an expression using equal factors.

Answer: _____ [1]

6. Write the inverse operation for $\boxed{18 \times 24 = 432}$

Answer: _____ [1]

7. Twenty-five students took the Mathematics examination. Five students received 'A' grades.

(a) Write the faction in its lowest term that represents the number of students who got 'A's' on the examination.

Fraction

(b) Write the fraction from 'a' as a percentage.

Percentage

(c) Write the percentage from 'b' as a decimal number.

Decimal number

8. Mr. Rolle drew this picture.

■ ■ ☐ ☐
■ ■ ☐ ☐
■ ■ ☐ ☐

Write one pair of equivalent fractions for Mr. Rolle's picture.

Answer: _____ [1]

9. Place an 'X' on the fraction that is written in its simplest form.

| $\frac{14}{21}$ | $\frac{4}{13}$ | $\frac{99}{121}$ | $\frac{25}{100}$ |

Answer: _____ [1]

10. Mark an 'X' on each letter in the box that has two lines of symmetry.

[2]

Use the figure below to answer question 11 (a) and (b).

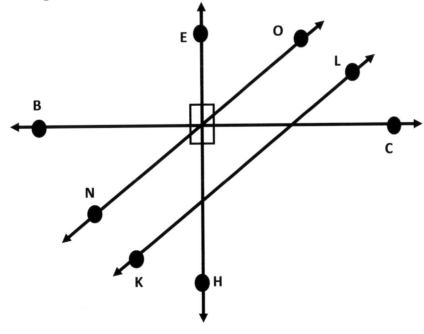

11. (a) Name a pair of perpendicular lines.

Answer: _____ [1]

(b) Name a pair of parallel lines.

Answer: _____ [1]

Use the angles below to answer questions 12(a) & 12(b).

(a) 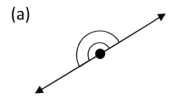   (b)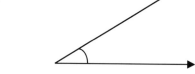

(c) 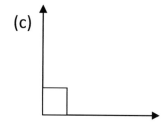   (d)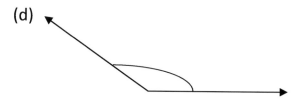

12. (a) Write the letter of the angle that has the smallest measurement.

Answer: _____ [1]

(b) Write the **NAME** of the angle with the greatest measurement.

Answer: _____ [1]

13. Write whether the two figures appear to be similar or congruent.

Answer: _____ [1]

14. Use the clock to answer question 14.

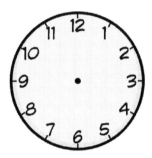

The time is 19:00 hours. Draw in the hands on the clock to show the time this would be on the twelve hour clock.

Answer: [1]

15. Complete the table to show the relationship between the units.

METRIC UNIT OF MASS		
MILLIGRAMS	GRAMS	KILOGRAMS
(a) 1 000		
(b)	1 000	

[2]

For Answer Key Go To:

http://greatminds.teachable.com/courses/glat-workbook-answer-keys/

MATHEMATICAL CONCEPTS – MAY 2014

1. Write five hundred eighty seven million, ninety five thousand, two hundred sixty four in:

   (a) Standard form:

   _____
   _____ [1]

   (b) Expanded form:

   _____
   _____ [2]

2. Write the reciprocal of $\frac{5}{9}$.

   Answer: _____ [1]

3. (a) Place an 'X' on the number in the box that is **NOT** a prime factor of 63.

   | 3 | 7 | 9 |

   (b) Write one other factor of 63 that is not listed in the box above.

   Answer: _____ [1]

4. Write the letter 'B' at the point on the ruler which shows 25 millimeters.

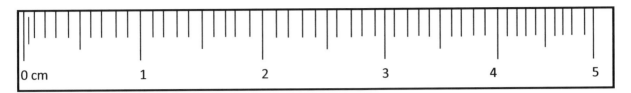

(Not Drawn to Scale)

Answer: [1]

Use the number line to answer questions 5. (a) & (b).

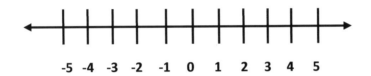

5. (a) Name the point on the line that is opposite of 2.

Answer: _____ [1]

(b) Write the number that is the complete opposite of itself.

Answer: _____ [1]

6. Place an 'X' on the number in the box that is divisible by both 3 and 5.

| 18 | 240 | 5 973 |

Answer: [1]

7. Angela drew this picture.

   ■ ■ ■ ☐ ☐ ☐
   ■ ■ ■ ☐ ☐ ☐
   ■ ■ ■ ☐ ☐ ☐

   Write one pair of equivalent fractions for Angela's picture.

   Answer: _____ [1]

8. (a) Read the equation then correctly insert the decimal point in the product to make the stamen true.

   $$4.36 \times 0.672 = 292992$$

   Answer: _____ [1]

   (b) From the equation $\boxed{84.50 \div 5 = 16.90}$ write the number that names the quotient.

   Answer: _____ [1]

9. Rewrite the date shown using the Systems International Format.

   $$\boxed{\text{January 10, 1967}}$$

   Answer: _____ [1]

10. (a) Read the pattern and then write the missing number on the line to complete it.

| 70 × 6 = 42 | 700 × 6 = 4200 | _____ × 6 = 42000 |

Answer: [1]

(b) Name the rule that was used to complete the pattern in 10 (a).

Answer: _____ [1]

11. Read the equation then, write down the value of 'Y'.

| Y − 26 = 24 |

Answer: _____ [1]

12. Write the symbols < or > on the line to compare the group of numbers.

| 217.997 _____ 29.979 _____ 219.997 |

Answer: [2]

Use the picture to answer question 13.

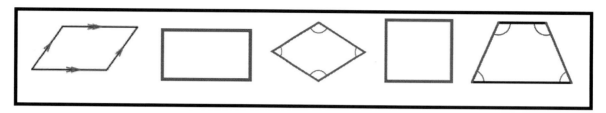

13. What special name is given to the group of figures shown?

Answer: _____ [1]

14. Write the name of the customary unit that would best measure the following:

(a) The capacity of a bathtub.

Answer: _____ [1]

(b) The weight of a newborn baby.

Answer: _____ [1]

Use the circle to answer questions 15. (a) & (b)

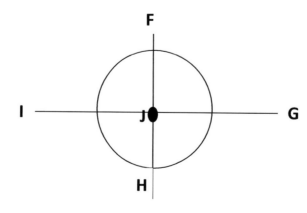

15. (a) Which part of the circle is line segment JH know as?

Answer: _____ [1]

15. (b) Write the letters from the circle which names the diameter.

Answer: _____ [1]

Use the chart to answer question 16.

FAVOURITE ACTIVITY	% OF STUDENTS
Watching TV	27%
Browsing the Internet	35%
Electronic games	23%
Board games	5%
Reading books	10%
150 SIXTH GRADERS WERE INTERVIEWED	

16. Name the type of graph that would be most appropriate to use for displaying the data shown in the table.

Answer: _____ [1]

For Answer Key Go To:

http://greatminds.teachable.com/courses/glat-workbook-answer-keys/

MATHEMATICAL CONCEPTS – MAY 2015

1. A number has 7 in the millions place, 6 in the hundred thousand place, 2 in the ten thousand place, 3 in the thousand place, 2 in the hundred place, 2 in the tens place and 2 in the ones place.

   (a) Write the number in standard form:
   _____ [1]

   (b) Round the number from 'a' to the nearest million:
   _____ [1]

2. (a) What is the square root of 81?

   Answer: _____ [1]

   (b) Write the equal factors for the square root of 81.

   Answer: _____ [1]

   Use the number line to answer question 3.

   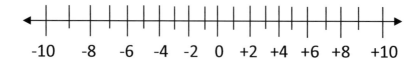

3. Write the letter 'P' at the point of (-3) on the number line. [1]

Use the factor tree to answer question 4.

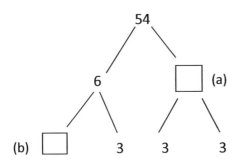

4. Write the missing numbers that are needed to complete the factor tree.

Answer: (a) _____ [1]
(b) _____ [1]

5. (a) From the term 10^6 write the numeral that is the base.

Answer: _____ [1]

(b) Calculate the complete value 10^6.

Answer: _____ [2]

6. Write the ratio 24:27 as a fraction in lowest terms.

Answer: _____ [2]

7. Insert the missing decimal point into the statement to make it correct.

$$2847 \times 6.4 = 182.208$$

Answer: _____ [1]

Use the models to answer questions 8(a) & 8(b).

8. (a) Write the pair of equivalent fractions that the model shows.

Answer: _____ [2]

(b) Write the pair of equivalent decimals that the models show.

Answer: _____ [2]

9. Read the algebraic expression then write down the variable.

$$7x \; q$$

Answer: _____ [2]

10. Write similar or congruent to describe each pair of objects.

(a)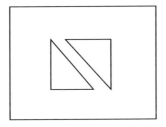

(b)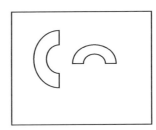

Answer: (a) _____ [1]

(b) _____ [1]

Use the figure to answer questions 11(a) & 11(b).

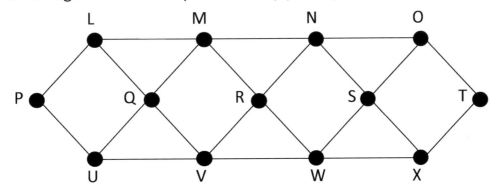

11. (a) What is the name given to the repeating pattern that is formed by the shapes shown in the diagram?

Answer: _____ [1]

(b) Write the name of the quadrilateral that is formed by figure PLQU.

Answer: _____ [1]

Use the line plot shown to answer question 12.

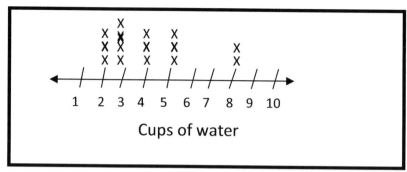

12. Write the number that is the outlier in the set of data shown.

Answer: _____ [1]

Use the circle to answer questions 13(a) & (b).

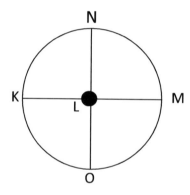

13. (a) Which part of the circle is line segment $\overline{LO}$ known as?

Answer: _____ [1]

(b) What is the name given to the continuous arc that helps to form circle 'L'.

Answer: _____ [1]

For Answer Key Go To:

http://greatminds.teachable.com/courses/glat-workbook-answer-keys/

MATHEMATICAL CONCEPTS – MAY 2016

1. Using the digits below, create the largest possible decimal number.

   | 4 | 6 | 8 | 2 |

   Answer: _____ [1]

2. The number **282,632** was rounded to **283,000**. Which place was the number rounded to?

   Answer: _____ [1]

3. Write the following number in the forms indicated below:

   80 000 000 + 7 000 000 + 500 000 + 30 000 + 400 + 90 + 2

   (a) Standard form:

   Answer: _____ [2]

   (b) Word form:

   Answer: _____
   _____
   _____ [1]

4. Circle the shape containing the digit '6' that carries the greatest value in the number.

   4235.60   6.2534   60.457   [1]

37

To answer question 5 use the symbols <, >, or =.

5. Insert the correct symbol in each of the empty figures below.

   $\frac{3}{4}$ ☐ $\frac{1}{5}$ ☐ 20% [2]

6. (a) From the set of numbers shown below, write down the following:

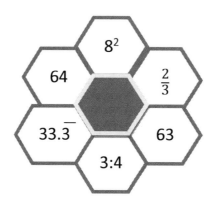

(i) A recurring decimal _____ [1]

(ii) A number divisible by both '3' and '7' _____ [1]

(iii) A ratio _____ [1]

(b) What is the name of the shape used to form the tessellation in part (a)?

Answer: _____ [2]

Use the table to answer both parts to question 7.

Brianne's Bowling Scores							
Games	1	2	3	4	5	6	7
Scores	78	90	78	88	78	90	70

7. From the numbers listed state the following:

(a) The mode:

Answer: _____[1]

(b) The median:

Answer: _____[1]

8. Insert the parenthesis in the correct position in the equation in order to make it true.

$$6 + 40 \div 10 = 10$$

Answer: _____[1]

Use the pictures below to answer question 9.

A.   B.

9. Write the correct letter of the polyhedron that represents a prism.

Answer: _____[1]

10. Fill in the blank section of the table below.

Solid Figure	Number of Edges	Number of Vertices
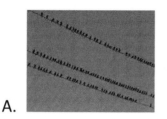		

11. The pictures below show two different types of electrical wires. For each picture name the geometrical line represented.

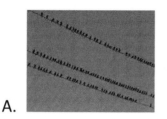
A.

B.

Answer: (a) _____[1]

Answer: (b) _____[1]

Use the clock to answer question 12. The new day has just begun.

12. (a) What is the time shown on the clock's face? Use a.m. or p.m. to complete the answer.

Answer: _____[1]

12. (b) Using your answer from the previous question, write the time in 24 hour notation.

Answer: _____[1]

Use the graph below to answer question 13.

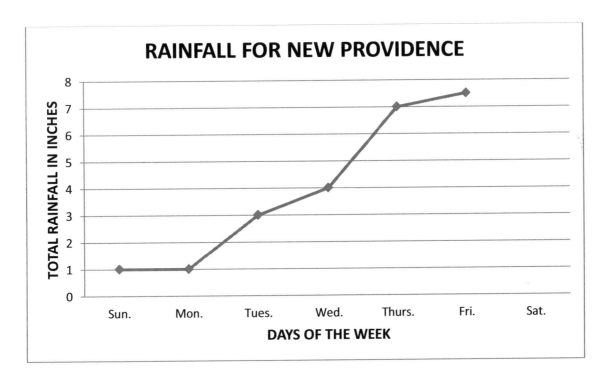

13. Which day of the week did it rain two more inches than the day before?

Answer: _____[1]

14. Which two days of the week was the rain levels the same? What was the rain level on these days?

Answer: _____
_____[2]

Use the Venn diagram below to answer both parts of question 15. The diagram shows the different modes of transportation students at King's College use to get to and from school.

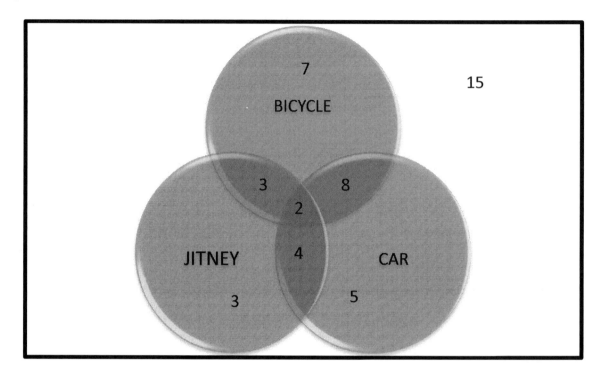

15.(a) What is the total number of students that use all three types of transportation to get to and from school?

Answer: _____[1]

15.(b) What is the total number of students that *DID NOT* use any of the types of transportation to get to and from school?

Answer: _____[1]

MATHEMATICAL CONCEPTS – MAY 2017

1. From the number $\boxed{267\ 319\ 852}$ write down the following:

(a) The value of digit in the thousands position

Answer _____[1]

(b) The value of the digit that is in the millions place.

Answer _____[1]

Use the picture to answer questions 2(a) and 2(b).

2.(a) What time is the clock showing? (Write your answer in standard time)

Answer _____[1]

2.(b) Write the standard time for three hours later.

Answer _____[1]

3. From the number | 0.61083 | write down the digit that has the greatest decimal place value.

Answer _____[1]

Use the graph to answer questions 3 (a) and 3(b).

4.(a) Express the shaded portion of the graph as a fraction.

Answer _____[1]

4.(b) Write the decimal that is represented by the unshaded section of the graph.

Answer _____[1]

5. Read the equation and then write the variable.

$$Z \div 2 + 12 = 18$$

Answer _____ [1]

6. Using the System International Format, rewrite the given date.

May 25, 2018

Answer _____ [1]

7.(a) What is the ratio of purple to blue buttons?

Answer _____ [1]

7. (b) Write the answer to 7(a) in its lowest reduced form.

Answer _____ [1]

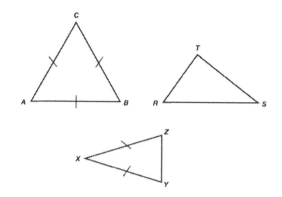

8. Draw lines of symmetry onto the triangles. [1]

9. Write down the symbols (<,> or =) on the blank lines to show their values.

(a) 72 inches _____ 5 yards

(b) 2kilograms _____ 2000 milligrams

Use the clock to answer questions 10 (a) and (b)

10. (a) What time is 11:30 p.m. on the 24 hour clock?

Answer _____[1]

10. (b) What time is 12:00 a.m. on the 24-hour clock?

Answer _____[1]

MATHEMATICAL CONCEPTS – MAY 2018

[5 tens]

[7 thousands]

[3 hundreths]

[6 ones]

1. Using the information shown on the place value cards, write the largest number that can be formed in:

   (a) Standard form

   _____ [1]

   (b) Expanded form

   _____ [1]

2. Using the fraction $\dfrac{23}{7}$ complete the following:

   (a) Write down the reciprocal for the fraction that is shown above.

   _____ [1]

   (b) Convert the original fraction to a mixed number.

   _____ [1]

3. Place an 'X' at the point on the ruler which shows 3.5 cm.

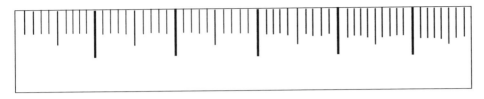

[1]

4. Using the number ☐2☐ as a base, complete the following:

   (a) Write 32 in exponential format.

   Answer: _____ [1]

   (b) Write 32 as an expression using equal factors.

   Answer: _____ [1]

Use the number line to answer questions 5 (a) and 5 (b).

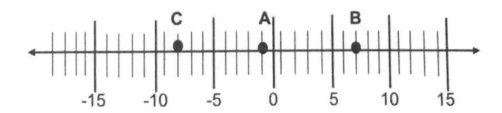

5. (a) State the integer that is represented by the letter 'C' on the number line.

   Answer: _____ [1]

5. (b) Write the opposite integer of the number that is represented by the letter "C" on the number line.

   Answer: _____ [1]

$$30.75 \div 5 = 615$$

6. Read the equation, then correctly insert the decimal point in the quotient to make the statement true.

   Answer: _____ [1]

7. From the equation $\boxed{428 - 234 = 194}$ write down the number that is the:

   (a) Difference _____ [1]

   (b) Minuend _____ [1]

   (c) Subtrahend _____ [1]

8. Use the chart to answer question 8(a), 8(b) and 8(c).

DAILY TEMPERATURES IN NASSAU						
84°	84°	87°	83°	64°	84°	87°

8(a). Arrange the numbers on the chart in ascending order. Write your answers in the empty boxes below.

DAILY TEMPERATURES IN NASSAU						

Using the completed data from section 8 (a), write down the following:

8(b). The number that is the median of the ordered set of numbers.

Answer: _____ [1]

8(c). The number that is the outlier in the ordered set of numbers.

Answer: _____ [1]

Use the street map to answer questions 9(a), 9(b) and 9(c).

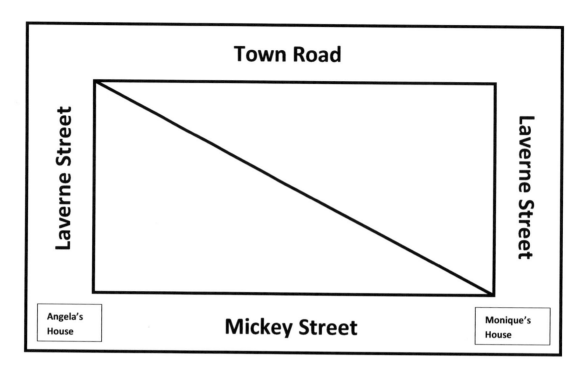

Name the geometric figure that is suggested by each of the following:

9(a). The path along Mackey Street that leads from Carol's house to Tanya's house.

Answer: _____ [1]

9(b). The property on which the church is built.

Answer: _____ [1]

9(c). The area that surrounds the basketball stadium.

Answer: _____ [1]

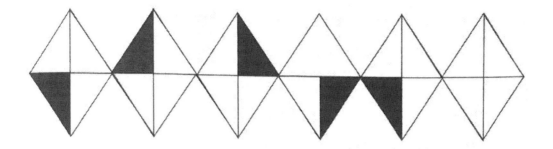

10. Tyler started to build the pattern shown above. Correctly shade the next figure in the pattern to complete it.

[1]

11. The difference between a number and 'm' and 18 is 39.

    Write an algebraic expression to outline the statement that is described above.

    Answer: _____ [1]

Use the spinner to answer questions 12(a) and 12(b).

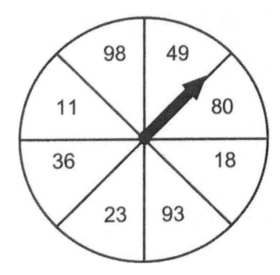

12(a) What is the probability of landing on a number that is less than 60?

Answer: _____ [1]

12(b) What is the probability of landing on a number that is divisible by 9?

Answer: _____ [1]

Use the graph to answer question 13.

(a)	
Romance	☺ ☺ ☺
Documentary	☺ ☺ ☺ ☺ ☺
Fiction	☺ ☺
Motivational	☺ ☺ ☺ ☺
Educational	☺ ☺ ☺ ☺ ☺ ☺ ☺
(b)	

13. Which sections of the graph are represented by the letters 'a' and 'b'?

(a) _____ [1]

(b) _____ [1]

MATHEMATICAL CONCEPTS – MAY 2019

1. Write the number $\boxed{942\ 236}$ in expanded form.

   _____ [1]

2. From the number $\boxed{470\ 108}$ write down the value of the digit '4'.

   Answer: _____ [1]

3. Write the number $\boxed{653\ 286\ 781}$ in short word form.

   Answer: _____ [1]

4. Round the number $\boxed{853.297}$ to the nearest

   (a) whole number

   _____ [1]

   (b) hundredths

   _____ [1]

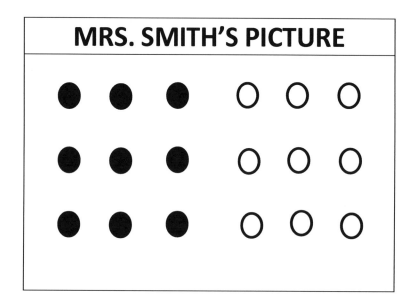

5. Write one pair of equivalent fractions for Mrs. Smith's picture.

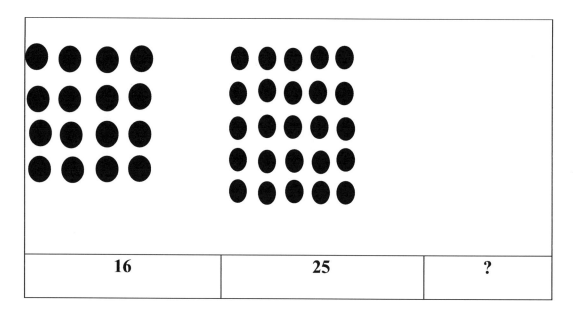

6. (a) Draw the missing dots in the empty box on the chart to complete the pattern. [1]

(b) Write the square number that is missing from the chart to complete it.

_____ [1]

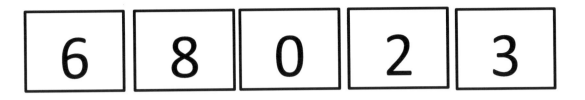

7. Place an 'X' on each number above that has **NO** line of symmetry. [2]

Use the shapes on the bag to answer questions 8(a) and 8(b).

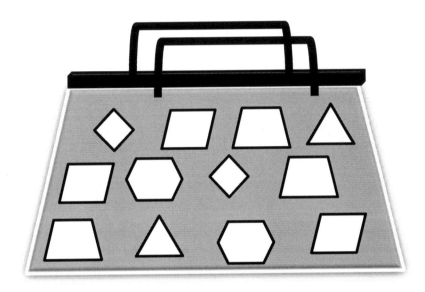

8. (a) What is the likelihood of lifting a trapezoid from the bag?

   Answer_____[1]

   (b) What is the likelihood of lifting a quadrilateral from the bag?

   Answer_____[1]

Use the pictures to answer questions 9 (a) and 9 (b).

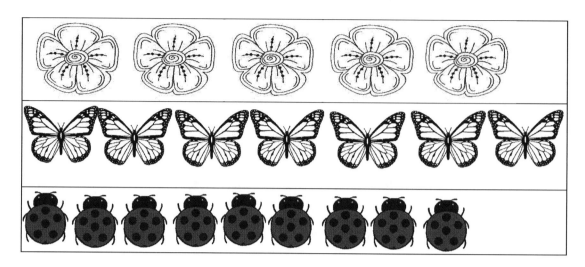

9. Write the ratio which shows each of the following:

   (a) flower to butterfly _____ [1]

   (b) Insects to flower__ _____ [1]

10. **Complete the chart below.**

NET	NAME OF SOLID FIGURE	NUMBER OF FACES	NUMBER OF VERTICES
△			

11. (a) Write the inverse operation for the equation $\boxed{169 + Q = 204}$

_____ [1]

58

11. (b) Write the variable from the equation in 11 (a)

_____[1]

12. Write <, > 0r = to compare the units.

   (a) 5 gallons ▢ 16 quarts

   (b) 800 mL ▢ 0.8 L [2]

Use the diagram to answer questions 13(a), 13(b) and 13(c).

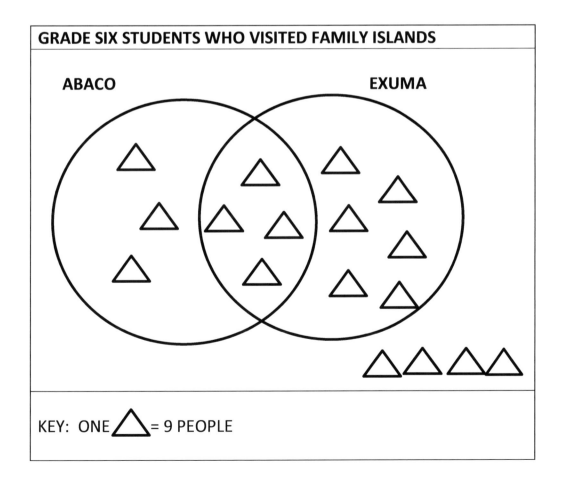

13. (a) What is the name by which the completed diagram above is known?

_____[1]

(b) Which group of students are represented by the triangles on the Outside of the circles?

_____[1]

(c) What do the four triangles in the section of the circles that overlap, mean?

_____[2]

COMPUTATION – MAY 2011

ADD:

1.   84
    + 632
    _____

2.   1 ☐ 2 3 3
    +   6 9 8 8
       2 6 ☐ 2 1
    _____
                       [1][3]

3. 8.46 + 47.4 + 7.839 = ☐

    Answer: _____[2]

4. (a) 62 mm + 26 mm = ☐

    Answer: _____[1]

   (b) Convert the answer from (a) into centimeters.

    Answer: _____[2]

SUBTRACT:

5.   6 5 8 9
    - 1 4 3 2
    ‾‾‾‾‾‾‾

6. $8,010.32 - $5,308.85 = _____

[1][3]

7. Estimate each number to the nearest thousand then solve the estimated equation.

   103 558 =
  - 64 671 =
  ‾‾‾‾‾‾‾

Answer: _____[3]

8. $\frac{10}{20} - \frac{3}{20} - \frac{5}{20} =$ ☐

Answer: _____[2]

MULTIPLY:

9. 7055 x _____ = 7055

    Answer:_____[1]

10. 57 x 3 x 22 = _____

    Answer: _____[1]

11. 23.4 x 0.53 = _____

    Answer: _____[1]

DIVIDE:

12. 9 | 630   13. 34 | 528.36

Answer: _____   Answer: _____

14. Find 25% of $84.00

Answer: _____[2]

15. $\frac{1}{5} + \frac{2}{3} \div \frac{1}{3} =$ _____

Answer: _____[4]

For Answer Key Go To:

http://greatminds.teachable.com/courses/glat-workbook-answer-keys/

COMPUTATION – MAY 2012

ADD:

1. 5034
    $+2654$
    $\overline{}$

2. $19.95 + $7.49 + $40.05 = ☐

[1] [2]

3. Round each quantity to the nearest dollar then find the estimated sum.

   $39.76 =
   + $8.49 =
   $\overline{}$

[3]

4. $\dfrac{2}{13} + \dfrac{13}{13} + 1\dfrac{4}{13} = $ ☐

   Write your answer in lowest terms.

   Answer: _____ [2]

SUBTRACT:

5. 8673
    -451
    $\overline{}$

6. 64836
    $-25☐09$
    $\overline{}$
    $3☐927$

[1] [4]

7. (a) 4.22 kg – 2.37 kg =

   Answer: _____ [2]

(b) Convert the answer from 'a' to grams.

Answer: _____ [2]

MULTIPY:

8. Complete the table.

INPUT	OUTPUT
4	?
?	169
6.7	?
Rule = X 13	

[3]

9. 789 x ☐ = 78900

Answer: _____ [1]

10. (a) Simplify. Show ALL working.

3 x (4 + 2) = (3 x 4) + (3 x 2)

Answer: _____ [2]

(b) Name the multiplication property that is demonstrated in the equation in (a).

Answer: _____ [1]

11.   508
    x 94
    ―――――

12. $\frac{2}{5}$ of 90 = ☐

Answer: _____

[2] [2]

13. Insert parentheses ( ) in the number sentence to make the statement true.

$$4^2 + 8 \div 4 \times 3 = 18$$

Answer: _____ [1]

DIVIDE:

14. $7\overline{)840}$

Answer: _____ [1]

15. $18\overline{)118}$

Answer: _____ [2]

16. $(1\frac{1}{8} + 1\frac{1}{2}) \div (2\frac{2}{5} - 1\frac{1}{10}) = $ ☐

Write the answer as a mixed number in lowest terms.

Answer: _____ [3]

For Answer Key Go To:

http://greatminds.teachable.com/courses/glat-workbook-answer-keys/

COMPUTATION – MAY 2013

ADD:

1. $\quad$ 7 5 0 4
    $+\quad$ 3 9 2
    _____

2. $\quad$ 6 2 4 7 3
    $+$ 2 6 5 4 4
    _____ [1] [2]

3. 567 + 94 - ☐ = 421 [2]

4. $\dfrac{9}{15} + \dfrac{5}{15} = $ ☐

5. $\dfrac{1}{2} + \dfrac{8}{12} + \dfrac{2}{3} = $ ☐

[2] [3]

SUBTRACT:

6. $\quad$ 8 6 3 4
   $-\quad$ 1 4 0 2
   _____

7. $\quad$ \$ 9 6 . 0 2
   $-$ \$ $\quad$ 4 . 8 1
   _____ [1] [2]

8. 236.07g – 9.879g = ☐

Answer: _____ [3]

9. $\dfrac{11}{3} - \dfrac{7}{3} = $ ☐

Answer: _____ [2]

MULTIPLY:

10. 5 0 1
   ×   7
   _____

11. 4 8 7 9
    × 9 0 8
    _____

[1] [3]

12. $\frac{1}{5} \times \frac{2}{9} = \boxed{}$

13. $1\frac{1}{4} \times 3\frac{1}{2} \times 2\frac{1}{3} = \boxed{}$

[1] [3]

DIVIDE:

14. $623 \div 100 = \boxed{}$

15. $25 \overline{) 180}$

Answer: _____ [1]

Answer: _____ [2]

16. $(4\frac{1}{4} + 2\frac{5}{6}) \div \frac{3}{8} = \boxed{}$

Answer: _____ [2]

17. If a=4 and b=7 complete the following equation

   $5a + b = \boxed{}$

Answer: _____ [2]

For Answer Key Go To:

http://greatminds.teachable.com/courses/glat-workbook-answer-keys/

COMPUTATION – MAY 2014

ADD:

1. 1 5 3 2
    \+   3 0 5
         4 1
    _____

2. 2 7 4 5 7
    \+ 1 8 2 9 2
    _____

    [1] [2]

3. 23.24 + 957.2 + 0.068 = ☐ [2]

4. $ 5 8 9 . 0 5
    \+ 1 3 0 . 9 6
    _____

5. $3\frac{1}{9} + 2\frac{2}{9} + \frac{5}{9} =$ ☐

    [2] [2]

6. $\frac{3}{4} + \frac{1}{10} + \frac{2}{5} =$ ☐ [3]

SUBTRACT:

7. $ 7 9 2 . 5 5
    \-   6 1 . 0 3
    _____

8. $ 9 0 0 6
    \- 5 3 0 7
    _____

    [1] [2]

9. $\frac{9}{17} - \frac{6}{17} =$ ☐

Answer: _____ [1]

10. $7\frac{5}{8} - 3\frac{1}{4} = \boxed{}$

Answer: _____ [3]

MULTIPLY:

11. $\begin{array}{r}9\,0\,1 \\ \times6 \\ \hline \\ \hline \end{array}$

12. $4.267 \times 10^2 = \boxed{}$

[1] [2]

13. $\begin{array}{r}4\,2\,7\,3 \\ \times8\,9 \\ \hline \\ \hline \end{array}$

14. $\frac{2}{3} \times \frac{5}{9} = \boxed{}$

[3] [1]

DIVIDE:

15. $3\overline{)3\,3\,6}$

Answer: _____ [1]

16. $21\overline{)5\,7\,8\,1}$

Answer: _____ [2]

17. $8 \times \frac{1}{4} \div \frac{1}{3} = \boxed{}$

Answer: _____ [3]

18. $93 - (42 \div 8) = \boxed{}$

Answer: _____ [3]

For Answer Key Go To:

http://greatminds.teachable.com/courses/glat-workbook-answer-keys/

COMPUTATION – MAY 2015

ADD:

1. 8 3 2 1 5
  + 0 6 0 7 4
  _____

2. 0 9 4 . 6 0 0
  + 0 0 5 . 2 6 8
    4 0 0 . 7 2 0
    _____

    _____ [1] [2]

3. $\frac{5}{7} + \frac{4}{7} = \square$

4. Hr. Mins. Sec.
     4   3 5   2 0
   + 4   2 7   3 2   [1] [3]
   _____

SUBTRACT:

5. 9 8 7 6
  − 2 4 0 3
  _____
  _____

6. 3 7 0 0 0
  − 1 5 6 4 2
  _____
  _____ [1] [2]

7. $526 - 431.92 = \square$

8. $13 - 9\frac{2}{3} = \square$

Answer: _____

Answer: _____ [2] [3]

MULTIPLY:

9. 2 1 0
    ×   8
    _____

10. 16 × 23 = ☐

   [1] [2]

11. 9 5 1
    × 2 6 7
    _____

12. 6 . 4 × 5 . 0 2 = ☐

   [3] [1]

DIVIDE:

13. 4 ⟌ 448

Answer: _____ [1]

14. 27 ⟌ 536.19

Answer: _____ [3]

15. $5\frac{3}{7} \div 12 =$ ☐

Answer: _____ [3]

16. $6\frac{1}{3} + \frac{4}{9} - (\frac{4}{5} \times \frac{1}{4}) =$ ☐

Answer: _____ [4]

For Answer Key Go To:

http://greatminds.teachable.com/courses/glat-workbook-answer-keys/

COMPUTATION – MAY 2016

ADD:

1. $\quad 2128$
    $+\underline{950}$

2. $\quad 24\square 6$
    $+\ 3851$
    $\underline{5650}$
    $11\square 67$
    $\underline{}$ [1] [2]

3. $5\frac{1}{3} + 6\frac{3}{4} = \square$

    Answer: _____

4. $3289 + 22 + 207 = \square$

    Answer: _____

    [3] [2]

SUBTRACT:

5. $\quad 9860$
    $-\underline{7759}$

6. $\quad 2183$
    $-\underline{852}$

    [1] [2]

7. $\frac{10}{4} - \frac{3}{4} = \square$

    Answer: _____

8. $2.285 - 0.012 = \square$

    Answer: _____

    [1] [2]

MULTIPLY:

9. 5 3 1
    × 1 1
    ———————

10. $4^3 \times 7^2 = \boxed{}$

[2] [3]

11. 25% of 240 = $\boxed{}$

12. $\dfrac{6}{5} \times \dfrac{5}{9} \times 8 = \boxed{}$

Answer: _____

Answer: _____

[2] [3]

DIVIDE:

13. $4 \overline{\smash{)}848}$

Answer: _____ [1]

14. $27 \overline{\smash{)}337.5}$

Answer: _____ [3]

EVALUATE:

15. $4 \times 6 - 15 \div 5 + 7 = \boxed{}$

Answer: _____ [3]

17. Find the value of 'a' in the following equations:

    12a = 156

    Answer: _____ [2]

18. $8\frac{1}{4} + \frac{3}{8} - \frac{6}{2} = \square$

    Answer: _____ [3]

For Answer Key Go To:

http://greatminds.teachable.com/courses/glat-workbook-answer-keys/

COMPUTATION – MAY 2017

ADD

1. 8 7 6 5 4
        9 7 1
    +   8
    _____

2. 3 2 7 5 9 0
       2 1 6 8
    +   4
    _____

[1][2]

3. $7 \frac{5}{8} + 9 \frac{1}{8} =$ ☐

4. $8.337 + 92 + 4.44 =$ ☐

Answer _____   Answer _____

[3][2]

SUBTRACT

     $ ¢

5. 7 6 1 . 2 5
    - 4 5 . 3 9
    _____

6. 9 0 5 2 7
    - 4 7 3 9 5
    _____

[1][2]

7. 9 3 5
    - 8 0 1
    _____

8. $\frac{5}{8} - \frac{1}{4} =$ ☐

Answer _____   Answer _____

[2][3]

MULTIPLY

9. ☐ X 17 = 1700

10. $48 \times \dfrac{3}{8} =$ ☐

Answer _____

Answer _____ [2][2]

11. If 'Y' = 9 and 'X' = 11
Calculate the following:

6x + 8Y = ☐

12.   9 1 3 5
    x   6 7 4
    ─────────

Answer _____

Answer _____ [2][3]

DIVIDE

13. 143 ÷ 11 = ☐

Answer _____ [1]

14. 9)573‾

Answer _____ [2]

15. $8 \overline{)6{,}947.63}$

Answer _____ [3]

16. $8\frac{3}{5} \div 2 = \boxed{}$

Answer _____ [3]

Evaluate:

17. $10 + 2.55 + 7 = \boxed{}$

Answer _____ [2]

For Answer Key Go To:

http://greatminds.teachable.com/courses/glat-workbook-answer-keys/

COMPUTATION – MAY 2018

ADD:

1. 5 4 1 7 3
  + 1 0 6 0 1
     4 4 2 6
  _____

2. $7,568.50 + $903.25 = ☐

Answer:_____ [1] [2]

3. $9\frac{2}{5} + \boxed{}\frac{1}{5} = 17\frac{\boxed{}}{5}$

Answer: _____

4. $2\frac{1}{7} + 1\frac{3}{14} + 4\frac{1}{2} = \boxed{}$

Answer: _____ [2] [3]

SUBTRACT:

5. 3 7 8 1 3
  −   4 0 2
  _____

6. $38.06 - 1.952 = \boxed{}$

Answer: _____ [1] [2]

7. 3.5 m − 206 cm = ☐

Answer: _____

8. $24 - 17\frac{4}{7} = \boxed{}$

Answer: _____ [3] [2]

MULTIPLY:

9. 2 0 2 0
    X   8
    _____

10. $2^4 \times 4^2 \times 10 = \square$

    Answer: _____ [1] [3]

11. 6 1.8
    X 7 0 2
    _____

12. 15 % of 120 = $\square$

    Answer: _____ [3] [2]

DIVIDE:

13. $\overset{11}{?\overline{)132}}$

    Answer: _____ [1]

14. $29\overline{)74506}$

    Answer: _____ [2]

EVALUATE:

15.

Fraction	Decimal	Percentage
$\frac{1}{4}$	(i) ?	25%
$1\frac{1}{5}$	1.20	(ii) ?

(i) _____ [1]

(ii) _____ [1]

16. Solve

$$16 - (8 \div 2) - \frac{3}{8} = \Box$$

Answer: _____ [3]

17. Write the numerical equation for the Roman numeral below.

$$\boxed{CM + D - M = CD}$$

Answer: _____ [2]

COMPUTATION – MAY 2019

ADD

1. $\quad$ 4 0 6 2

    + 4 9 3 5

    _____

    _____

2. $\quad$ 7 3 5 1

    + 3 7 0 9

    _____

    _____

    [1] [2]

3. $23.78 + \boxed{} + 1.30 = 74.08$ $\qquad$ [2]

4. $\quad$ 5 7 0 8

    + 4 6 9 7

    _____

    _____

5. $\dfrac{2}{5} + \dfrac{1}{4} = \boxed{}$

    [2] [2]

SUBTRACT

6. 8 7 5 9
    - 6 5 8
    _____

    _____

7. $ ¢
    3 0 2 . 1 6
    - 1 8 3 . 0 7
    _____

    _____

    [1] [2]

8. 17.4 kg - 500 g = ☐

    Answer=_____

9. 8 - $4\frac{3}{7}$ = ☐

    Answer=_____

    [3] [2]

MULTIPLY

10. $356 \times 10^2 =$ ☐

11. $57 \times 90 =$ ☐

Answer=_____

Answer=_____

[2] [3]

12. $\frac{2}{3}$ of 240 = ☐

Answer=_____

[2]

DIVISION

13.

$7 \overline{)637}$

Answer=_____[1]

14.

$16 \overline{)154.4}$

Answer =_____[3]

EVALUATE:

15.

FRACTION	DECIMAL	PERCENTAGE
$\frac{1}{4}$	(i)	25%

(i) _____[1]

16. Solve

$$4^2 - (12 \div 3) + \frac{2}{9} = \Box$$

Answer=_____[3]

For Answer Key Go To:
http://greatminds.teachable.com/courses/glat-workbook-answer-keys/

APPLICATION – MAY 2011

1. The Bahamas National Trust volunteers worked 1,965 volunteer service hours this year. Last year they worked 1,890 total volunteer service hours.

   (a) What is the total number of hours worked in both years?

   Answer: _____[2]

   (b) How many more hours were worked this year compared to last year?

   Answer: _____[2]

2. The conference room was arranged with 20 rows and 12 chairs in each row. There were an additional 10 chairs at the presenter's table. What was the total number of chairs in the conference room?

Answer: _____[2]

3. Brianne has 9 coins that have a total value of 65 cents. What combination of coins does Brianne have?

Answer: _____[2]

4. The string on Joey's kite is 42.5 inches long. Ashton's kite string is 3.5 times as long as Joey's kite string. How long is Ashton's kite string?

Answer: _____[2]

5. Anna's basketball camp had 345 participants. One third of the camp participants were boys. How many girls attended the camp?

Answer: _____[2]

6. A box of markers contains 12 yellow, 6 green and 8 blue markers. What is the probability of choosing a yellow marker from the box? Express your answer in its lowest terms.

Answer: _____[2]

Use the diagram to answer question 7.

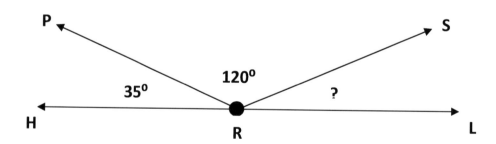

7. Calculate the size of ∠ SRL unknown angle.

Answer: _____[2]

8. Megan needs 2,500ml of chicken souse so each of her guests will have the same amount. How many liters of chicken souse does Megan have to make to have 2,500 ml?

Answer: _____ [2]

9. Ashley and her family are on vacation. They are 135 miles from their destination. If they are travelling 60 miles per hour, how long will it take them to get there?

Answer: _____ [3]

10. The Pratt family drove 205 miles from Burnt Ground to Clarence Town and 238 miles to return home. In Clarence Town they drove 97 miles while sightseeing.

(a) The Pratt's van can travel an average of 27 miles on 1 gallon of gas. How many gallons of gas did they use for their trip?

Answer: _____[2]

(b) If the cost of gasoline is $6.99 per gallon how much did the Pratt's spend on gas for the entire trip?

Answer: _____[2]

(c) The Pratt's allocated $100.00 for gas. How much more money was needed to cover the gas bill?

Answer: _____[1]

11. Theatre tickets are sold at a cost of $18.95 each.

(a) Susan sold $227.40 worth of tickets on Friday. How many tickets did she sell?

Answer: _____ [2]

(b) Susan has an additional ten tickets to sell. What would be Susan's total intake after all of her tickets are sold?

Answer: _____ [2]

Use the chart to answer question 12(a) and (b).

ISLAND	TOTAL POPULATION	MALES	FEMALES	NUMBER OF HOUSEHOLDS
NEW PROVIDENCE	210,832	101,610	109,222	59,707
ABACO	13,170	6,711	6,459	3,929

12. (a) How many more persons live in New Providence than in Abaco?

Answer: _____ [2]

(b) Calculate the difference between the total number of males and females.

Answer: _____[2]

Use the graph to answer question 13.

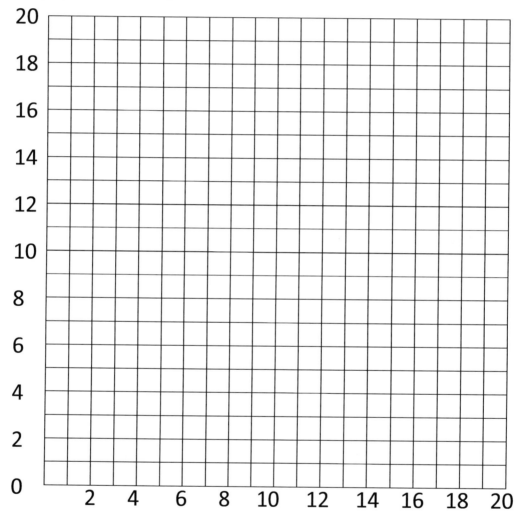

13. (a) Plot the following points on the graph then connect them.
       (i)   (5,10)   (ii)   (10,3)
       (iii)   (10,18)   (iv)   (15,10)

[4]

(b) Write the name of the quadrilateral that is formed when the lines are joined together.

Answer: _____ [2]

For Answer Key Go To:

http://greatminds.teachable.com/courses/glat-workbook-answer-keys/

APPLICATION – MAY 2012

1. In the last election 3 215 persons registered to vote at the post office, 879 persons registered at the clinics and 6 072 persons registered at the malls. Calculate the total number of persons who registered to vote.

   Answer: _____ [2]

2. Game Star members spend $58 034.00 buying electronic games annually. Of this total, $37 261.48 is spent on hand held games. How much do they spend on other electronic games each year?

   Answer: _____ [2]

Use the information below to answer questions 3. (a) and (b).

GAMES	ADULTS	CHILDREN
Softball	$5.00	$2.00
Soccer	$6.00	$2.50
Basketball	$7.00	$3.50

3. Mr. and Mrs. Sands and their three children paid a total of $24.50 for tickets.

(a) How much change would Mr. Sands get if he paid the cashier with two twenty-dollar bills?

Answer: _____ [2]

(b) Based on their purchase, which game does the Sands family plan to see?

Answer: _____ [2]

Use the picture to answer questions 4 (a) & (b).

BANANA SALE
35 cents each
OR
6 for $1.79

4. Mayaguana Mart has a sale on bananas. Mr. Kelly, the grocer, has 489 single bananas in stock.

(a) How many bunches of six bananas can he sell at the sale price?

Answer: _____ [2]

(b) If he sold all his bananas at the regular price of 35c each what would be his total intake?

Answer: _____ [2]

5. Destiny picked $5\frac{3}{4}$ pounds of guavas. She used $3\frac{5}{6}$ pounds of the guavas to make a duff. How many pounds of guavas did she have left?

Answer: _____ [2]

6. There are 24 hours in a day. The number of hours that are left in the day is equivalent to $\frac{1}{3}$ of the day. How many hours are left in the day?

Answer: _____ [2]

7. Eastwood farm has a rectangular vegetable garden that is 20.2m long and 7m wide. A fence that measures 23.5m long by 10m wide was placed around the garden. What is the difference between the area of the garden and the enclosed area of the fence?

Answer: _____ [3]

8. Jane has to be at work by 8:00 a.m. It takes her 25 minutes to get dressed, 15 minutes to eat and 40 minutes to drop the children off and arrive at work.

(a) How long does it take Jane to complete the morning chores? Record your answers in hours and minutes.

Answer: _____ [2]

(b) What is the latest time that Jane should get up if she is to arrive at work on time?

Answer: _____ [2]

Use the diagram to answer question 9.

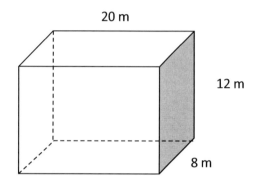

9. Find the volume of the prism

Answer: _____ [2]

10. Robyn left the tap on at home. If 180 liters of water run out of the tap every 30 seconds. How long will it take for 150 liters of water to run out of the tap?

Answer: _____ [2]

11. Keisha is older than Tonia, Tonia is younger than Joshua, Joshua is younger than Keisha but older than Tonia and Eden is the oldest of the group. Arrange the names of each person in the group from oldest to youngest.

Answer: _____ [2]

Use the spinner to answer question 12.

This is Celia's spinner.

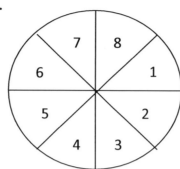

12. If Celia spins each number on the spinner once which of the following probabilities would be equivalent to $\frac{1}{4}$?

(a) P (odd numbers)
(b) P (numbers less than 3)
(c) P (numbers greater than 3)
(d) P (number 9)

Answer: _____ [1]

Use the Venn diagram to answer question 13. (a), (b), (c) and (d).

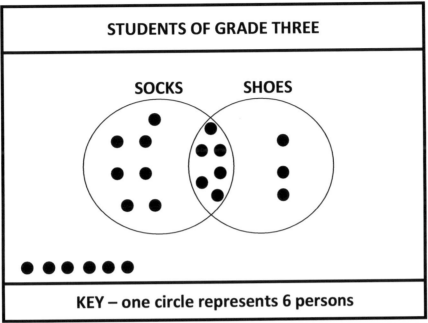

13. (a) How many persons wore shoes?

Answer: _____ [1]

(b) How many persons wore socks and shoes?

Answer: _____ [1]

(c) How many persons were counted altogether?

Answer: _____ [1]

Use the graph to answer question 14.

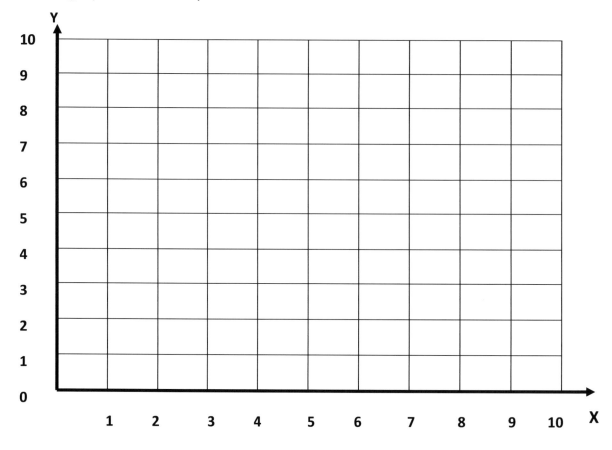

14. (a) Graph a triangle with vertices (1,4) (3,4) (1,7) and label it 'a'. [2]

(b) Transform the triangle to the vertices (3,4) (3,6) (6, 6) and label it 'b' [2]

(c) Name the transformation that occurred.

Answer: _____ [1]

For Answer Key Go To:

http://greatminds.teachable.com/courses/glat-workbook-answer-keys/

APPLICATION – MAY 2013

1. The Spring concert at Step-Above 10 Academy lasted for 55 minutes. The band played for 18 minutes and the choir sang for 23 minutes. The recorder recital group was the final item on the programme. How much time did the recorder recital group have to complete their selection?

   Answer: _____ [2]

2. Jill has six different colored sweaters and four different pairs of slacks. How many different outfits can she pair together?

   Answer: _____ [1]

3. Jennifer's bag of marbles has 5 blue marbles, 10 white marbles, 40 green marbles and 25 orange marbles.

(a) Write a fraction mathematical sentence to show the possibility of picking a blue, white or orange marble from the bag, at the same time, without looking?

Answer: _____ [2]

(b) Convert the numbers in the mathematical sentence from 'a' to their lowest terms then solve the equation. Show **ALL** working.

Answer: _____ [2]

4. A right angle triangle has a second angle of 60° and an unkown angle.

   (a) Sketch and label the triangle described above.

   [1]

   (b) Calculate the unknown angle.

   Answer: _____ [2]

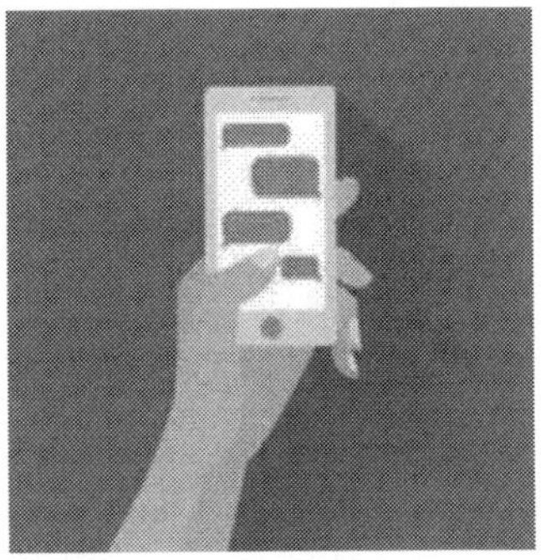

5. BSM Communications charges $0.05 for every text. Dajah sent 426 texts. What was the total amount of money that Dajah spent on texts?

   Answer: _____ [2]

6. Andre and his mother had lunch at the Fish Fry. Together, they spent $75.00 for their meals and they gave an additional 15% tip to the server. What was the total amount of money they spent?

Answer: _____ [2]

7. Nancy read for 7/10 of an hour on Monday and $3/4$ of an hour on Tuesday.

(a) How many minutes did Cheryl read altogether?

Answer: _____ [3]

(b) Convert the answer from 'a' to hours and minutes.

Answer: _____ [1]

8. Kay left her office at 1:00 pm. She returned to the office $3\frac{1}{4}$ hours later. At what time did Kay return to her office?

Answer: _____ [2]

9. Twenty-eight students from the fourth grade class at Adelaide Primary School visited the National Museum. The total cost of tickets for the trip was $276.38.

(a) What was the cost of each ticket?

Answer: _____ [2]

(b) The total bill was paid with three hundred dollar notes. How much change did the school receive?

Answer: _____ [2]

10. Bridgette is making guava jam. The recipe requires $8\frac{3}{4}$ cups of sugar. She poured $7\frac{1}{2}$ cups of sugar from the first bag and then she opened a new bag of sugar. How many cups of sugar does she need?

Answer: _____ [2]

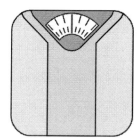

11. Angela weighs 164.6 kilograms. Last year she weighed 134.4 kilograms.

(a) How many kilograms did Angela gain?

Answer: _____ [2]

(b) Convert the answer from 'a' to grams.

Answer: _____ [1]

Use the graph to answer question 12, parts (a), (b) and (c).

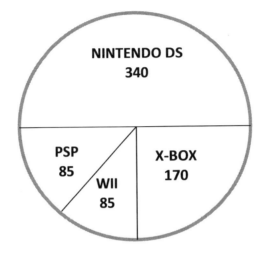

12. There are 680 students at Walter Parker School. The graph shows the number of students who own electronic games and the type of game they own.

(a) What percentage of the students owned an X-box?

Answer: _____ [1]

(b) Calculate the total number of students who owned an X-box and a Wii game.

Answer: _____ [3]

(c) Find the difference between the number of students who own a Nintendo and a PSP game.

Answer: _____ [2]

Use the graph to answer questions 13. (a), (b) and (c).

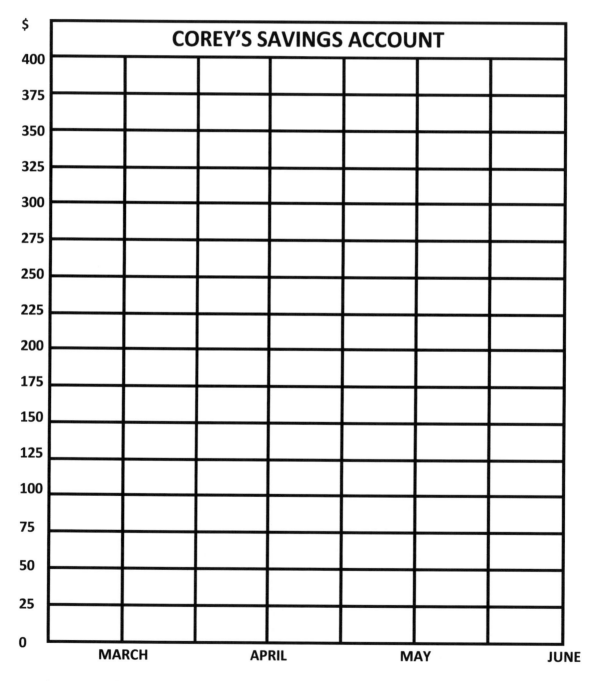

The table shows the money on Corey's savings account.

March	$250.00
April	$150.00
May	$325.00
June	$175.00

13. (a) Show this data on the graph. [2]

(b) Between which two months did Corey's account increase the most?

Answer: _____ [1]

(c) What was the overall increase between the two months named in 'b'?

Answer: _____ [2]

For Answer Key Go To:

http://greatminds.teachable.com/courses/glat-workbook-answer-keys/

APPLICATION – MAY 2014

Use the table to answer question 1.

ATTENDANCE AT FAMFEST BAHAMAS 2014	
Friday night	1 654
Saturday night	4 230
Sunday night	649

1. Calculate the total number of persons who attended the 2014 family festival event.

   Answer: _____ [2]

2. The regular price of an Ipod is $280. Paula purchased one at the sale price. How much money did she save?

   Answer: _____ [2]

3. Quentin left Andros at 10:20 a.m. and arrived in Nassau at 11:35 a.m.

(a) Calculate the time it took Quentin to travel to Nassau from Andros.

Answer: _____ [1]

(b) Quentin took an additional half hour to get from the airport to the hotel. At what time did Quentin arrive at the hotel?

Answer: _____ [2]

4. Mr. Mackey bought 32 Math books at a cost of $18.50 each.

(a) What was the total amount of money that Mr. Mackey spent for the books?

Answer: _____ [2]

(b) When Mr. Mackey paid his bills he received $8.00 in change. How much money did he give the cashier?

Answer: _____ [2]

5. Robyn, Kristy, Tenaj and Joey bought 9 yards of string to share equally for their kite tails.

(a) Calculate the amount of string each friend received.

Answer: _____ [2]

(b) Round the answer from 5(a) to the nearest whole number.

Answer: _____ [1]

6. Ashton has 120 marbles in a bag. 25% of the marbles are green.

(a) How many green marbles does Ashton have in total?

Answer: _____ [2]

(b) How many of Ashton's marbles are not green?

Answer: _____ [2]

7. Nicholas' mother baked 2 dozen cupcakes. She sold 21 of them. What percentage of the cupcakes did she have left?

Answer: _____ [3]

8. Brianne is 10 years old and her brother Jarrod is 5 years old.

(a) Draw an extending pattern to show the progression of Brianne and Jarrod's age over an eight year period.

Answer: [2]

Brianne 10 yrs.								
Jarrod 5 yrs.								

(b) Which two ages from the table will give a combined age of 31 years?

Answer: _____ [1]

9. At Michelle's birthday party $\frac{8}{12}$ of the cake was shared with family and friends. The next day she took $\frac{1}{2}$ of what was left to school. What fraction of the cake was taken to school?

Answer: _____ [3]

10. During the summer break Manny took on a summer job cleaning windows, to make extra money.

(a) If Manny cleans 9 windows in 60 minutes, how many windows will he be able to clean 20 minutes?

Answer: _____ [2]

(b) Convert the answer from 10(a) to hours and minutes.

Answer: _____ [1]

RECIPE FOR ONE CHOCOLATE CAKE
- 4 eggs (one egg weighs 50 grams)
- 200 grams butter
- 250 grams of sugar
- 2 tablespoons of baking powder
  (1 tablespoon of baking powder weighs 12 grams)
- 24 grams of dark chocolate
- 850 grams of flour

11. What would be the total mass of the chocolate cake when all the ingredients would have been combined?

Answer: _____ [2]

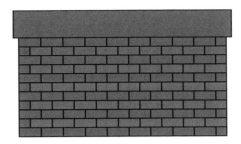

12. Mr. Johnson's wall is 106 feet long and 8.3 feet high. He paid his son 25 cents per square foot to paint the wall.

(a) Find the square footage of the wall.

Answer: _____ [2]

(b) What was the total amount of money that Mr. Johnson paid his son for painting the wall?

Answer: _____ [2]

Use the graph to answer question 13 (a), (b) and (c).

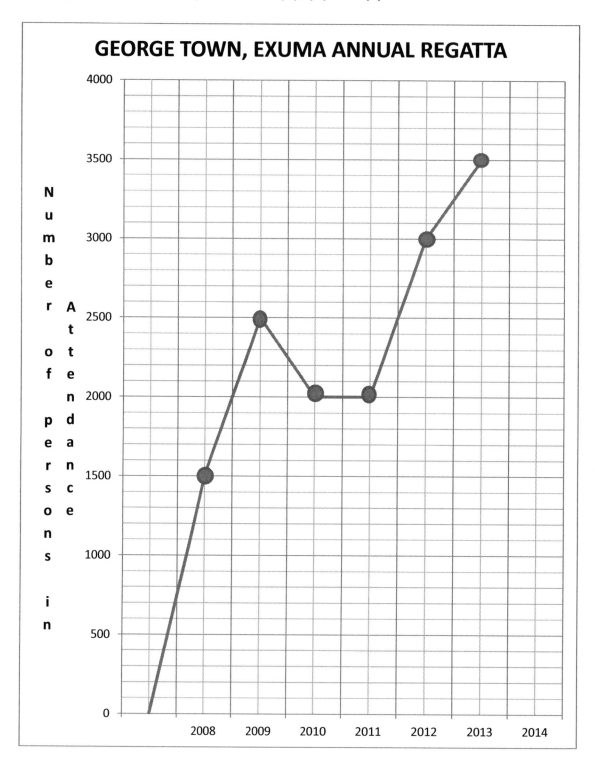

The graph shows the number of persons who attended the George Town Regatta over a six year period.

13. (a) In which two years were the attendance at the regatta constant?

Answer: _____ [1]

(b) What is the range of the attendance at the regatta?

Answer: _____ [1]

(c) Find the average attendance for the six years of the regatta.

Answer: _____ [1]

For Answer Key Go To:

http://greatminds.teachable.com/courses/glat-workbook-answer-keys/

APPLICATION – MAY 2015

Bethany made a deposit at the local bank. This is what the deposit slip looked like.

BAHAMIAN NOTES		U.S. NOTES	
5 × 1	5.00	2 × 1	2.00
4 × 5	20.00	1 × 5	5.00
3 × 10	30.00	3 × 10	30.00
7 × 20	140.00	5 × 20	100.00
2 × 50	100.00	6 × 50	300.00
1 × 100	100.00	3 × 100	300.00
TOTAL		TOTAL	

1. (a) Calculate the total amount that is on each of Bethany's deposit slips.

    Answer: Bahamian notes: _____ [1]
    U.S. notes: _____ [1]

    (b) Calculate the total amount of money that Bethany deposited at the local bank.

    Answer: _____ [2]

    (c) Calculate the difference between the two currencies that were deposited.

    Answer: _____ [2]

2. A taxi travels at a speed of 50 miles per hour. How far will it travel in five hours?

Answer: _____ [2]

3. The subtotal of the Rolle's grocery bill is $265.00.

(a) What would be the total bill when 12 % VAT is added to the bill?

Answer: _____ [2]

(b) Round the total bill to the nearest hundred dollars.

Answer: _____ [2]

4. Admission to Galleria Cinema is $5.50 per student. If 82 students paid, how much money will be collected for admission?

Answer: _____ [2]

5. Ramon is 1/3 of his mom's age. If his mom is 42 years old, how old is Ramon?

Answer: _____ [2]

6. Mary needs $12\frac{1}{2}$ lbs of sheep tongue to make souse. She has $6\frac{2}{3}$ lbs. How much more sheep tongue does she need?

Answer: _____ [3]

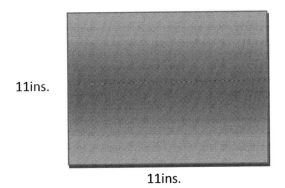

11ins.

11ins.

7. (a) Find the perimeter of the square.

Answer: _____ [1]

(b) Find the area of the square.

Answer: _____ [2]

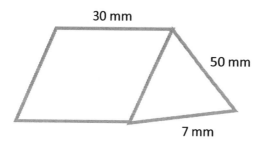

8. Find the volume of the triangular prism shown.

   Answer: _____ [2]

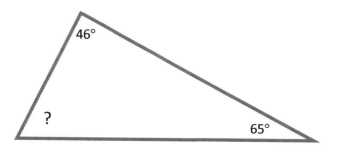

9. A triangle has two angles measuring 46° and 65°. What is the measure of the third angle?

   Answer: _____ [2]

Use the schedule of the Jitney to answer question 10.

START	STOP	INTERVALS
6:00 a.m.	8:00 a.m.	Every 15 minutes
8:00 a.m.	12:00 noon	Every half hour

10. Calculate the number of stops the jitney makes between 7:00 a.m. and 11:00 a.m.

    Answer: _____ [3]

11. A group of 6th grade students were surveyed. 32 liked Reggae, 27 liked Hip Hop and 35 liked Calypso. Using this information answer the questions that follow.

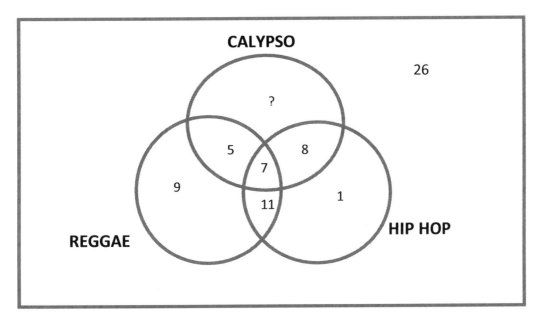

(a) How many students enjoyed Calypso only?

Answer: _____ [2]

(b) What was the total number of students that enjoyed all three types of music?

Answer: _____ [2]

(c) What was the total number of students that were surveyed?

Answer: _____ [2]

Use the graph to answer question 12(a) and (b).

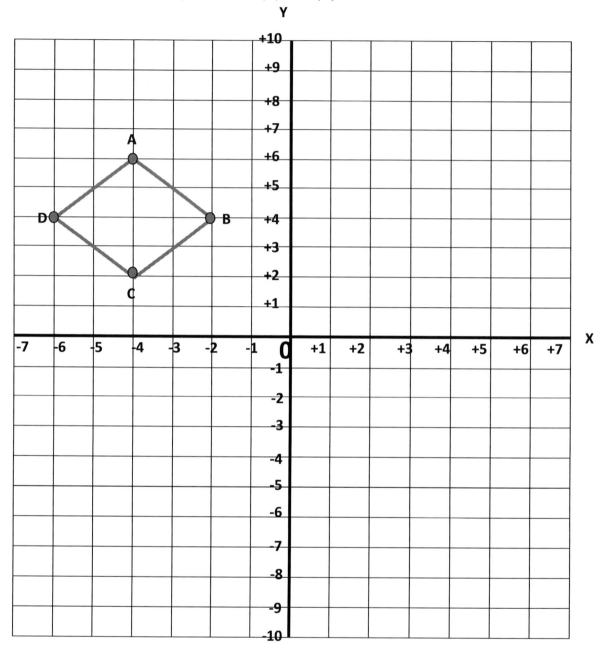

(a) Name the coordinates for each point plotted in the figure shown on the grid.

(a) _____

(b) _____

(c) _____

(d) _____   [2]

(b) Use the coordinates given to plot the points and translate the figure shown to a new location on the grid.

(+4, -2)

(+6, -4)

(+4, -6)

(+2, -4)   [2]

For Answer Key Go To:
http://greatminds.teachable.com/courses/glat-workbook-answer-keys/

APPLICATION – MAY 2016

1. Rickelle's mother paid $265.85 for her books, $126.13 for supplies and an additional $50 for the technology lab fee.

   (a) Calculate the total amount of money that Rickelle's mother paid for all of her school equipment.

   Answer: _____[1]

   (b) If Rickelle's mother used five one hundred dollar notes to pay her bill, how much change will she get back?

   Answer: _____ [2]

2. A reporter for The Tribune wrote an article each week for five years straight. At the end of the fifth year, what was the total number of articles the reporter wrote?

   Answer: _____[2]

3. Nicholas bought 273 gumballs. He shared the gumballs equally between three containers. How many gumballs did Nicholas place in each container?

   Answer: _____[2]

4. Sharon received a box from her grandmother in Long Island containing 18 dillies, 50 juju's, 9 mangolas and 13 avocados.

   1. What is the total number of fruits that Sharon received in her box?

      Answer: _____[2]

   2. What is the probability of selecting a dilly and an avocado from the box?

      Answer: _____[1]

5 ft. ?

5. The length of a garden is 3 times its width. The width of the garden is 5 feet. Find the perimeter of the garden.

Answer: _____[3]

6. Nicole makes hot patties that each have a mass of 126 grams. How many grams is 27 hot patties?

Answer: _____[2]

7. Great Minds Academy raises $600 to purchase new books for four local school libraries. To date they have purchased $450 worth of books. What percentage of the total overall amount have they used to purchase books?

Answer: _____[2]

8. Angela has 23 meters of ribbon. She gave $13\frac{3}{7}$ meters of the ribbon to Anna. How much ribbon does Angela have left?

Answer: _____[3]

9. Step-Above 10 has a population of 500 students. Of this amount, 45% are boys. How many boys attend Step-Above 10?

Answer: _____[2]

10. Each day Olivia studies for 3 hours and 20 minutes while Jarrod studies for 4 hours and 10 minutes. Calculate the difference between Olivia and Jarrod's study times.

Answer: _____[2]

11. Joey spent a total of $123.00 for his basketball and basketball shoes. The basketball costs $35.67. How much money did Joey spend on his basketball shoes?

Answer: _____[2]

Use the graph to answer questions 12(a) & (b).

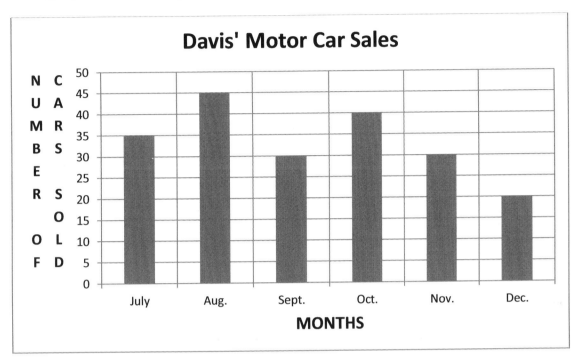

12.(a) What was the total number of cars sold from July to December?

Answer: _____[2]

12. (b) Calculate the mean for the total number of cars sold during the months of August to December?

Answer: _____[2]

Using the data from the table and the graph, answer question 13 parts a, b & c.

FAVOURITE PETS OF GRADE 3 BURROWS STUDENTS	
Dog	½
Cat	1/8
Bird	¼
Other	?

13.(a) Write the fractions from the table in the correct positions on the pie graph to complete it.

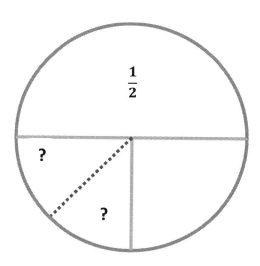

Answer: [2]

13. (b) Write the fraction represented by the section outlined in the dotted lines on the pie graph.

Answer: _____[2]

13. (b) Write a pair of equivalent fractions shown in the pie graph.

Answer: _____[2]

Use the graph to answer question 14(a), (b) and (c).

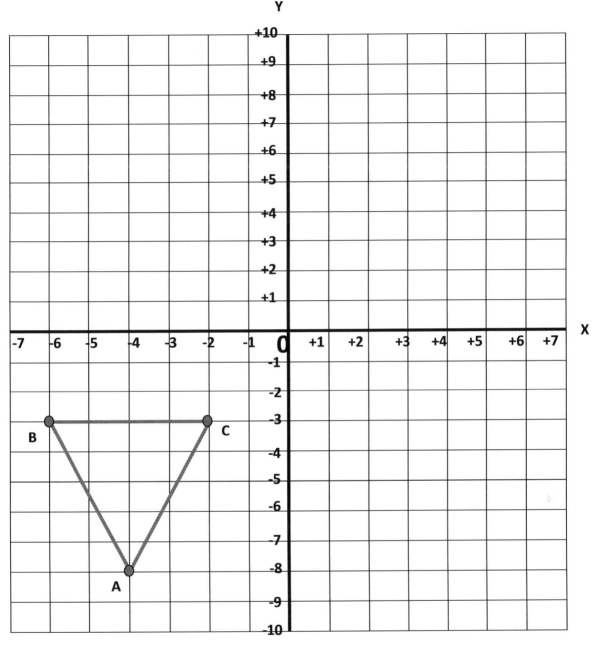

14. (a) Name the coordinates for each point plotted in the figure shown on the grid.

　(i)　_____

　(ii)　_____

　(iii)　_____

[3]

14. (b) Use the coordinates given to plot the points and transform the figure shown to a new location on the grid.

　(-2, +3)

　(-6, +3)

　(-4, +8)

[3]

14. (c) Name the transformation that took place with the figure in (b) to create the new figure.

Answer: _____ [2]

For Answer Key Go To:

http://greatminds.teachable.com/courses/glat-workbook-answer-keys/

APPLICATION – MAY 2017

SEA WORLD TICKET PRICES		
FAMILY PACKAGE	ADULT	CHILD
5(+) = $480	$125	$70
4(-) = $375		

A family of 5 paid to visit Sea World. There are 2 adults and 3 children.

1. (a) Is it cheaper to purchase the Family Package or purchase individual tickets? Show your working.

   Answer _____[3]

1. (b) They purchased the individual tickets and paid with $500. What is their change?

   Answer _____[2]

2. Maria works at Bahamar. She valet parks visitor cars. The car lot has 15 rows where 9 cars can fit in each row. Calculate the maximum amount of cars to be valeted.

Answer_____[1]

3. Natalie and Michael were asked to bathe the dogs at their Pet store in one day. There are 222 dogs and it must be completed in 10 hours. If they bathed 25 dogs in one hour how long would it take to complete all?

Answer_____[3]

4. Subway prepared 4,520 sandwiches for a Business function. They had 40 staff members on hand. How many sandwiches were divided amongst each staff member?

Answer_____[2]

5. Jonathan is an event coordinator and has to seat 2550 persons at his upcoming Bridal party. Each table he has sits 15 people. How many tables would he need to have everyone seated?

Answer_____[2]

$$75 + 20 \div 5$$

Zora and James were asked to work a problem. Zora's answer was 19 and James' answer was 79.

6. (a) What type of problem is being presented?

Answer _____[2]

6. (b) Which student is correct?

Answer _____[1]

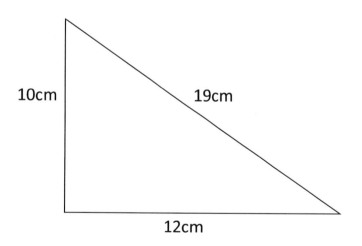

7. (a) Calculate the perimeter of the triangle.

Answer _____[2]

7. (b) Find the area of the triangle

Answer _____[2]

8. Captain Glynn took a boat trip to Grand Bahama at 6 p.m on Sunday. The trip lasted two and a half days.

(a) Which day did Glynn arrive back to Nassau?

Answer _____[2]

(b) At what time did Glynn arrive home?

Answer _____[2]

9. Mr. Steed's students took half an hour to prepare their science projects every school day including Saturday. They did this for 2 weeks. Calculate the total time they spent preparing for the Science Fair.

Answer _____[3]

10. Stephen Dillet Primary school has 17 classrooms. There are 5 computers in each classroom and 5 tablets. There are 200 students. Only 60% of the students use the computers. 40% use the tablets.

(a) Calculate the percentage of students that uses computers.

Answer _____[2]

(b) Calculate the total amount of computers in all classrooms.

Answer _____[2]

(c) Calculate the percentage of students that use tablets.

Answer _____[2]

(d) Calculate the amount of tablets in all classrooms.

Answer _____[2]

For Answer Key Go To:

http://greatminds.teachable.com/courses/glat-workbook-answer-keys/

APPLICATION – MAY 2018

MR. THOMPSON'S MANGO STAND	
DAY OF THE WEEK	NUMBER OF MANGOS SOLD
Monday	345
Tuesday	?
Wednesday	175
Thursday	420
Friday	190
TOTAL NUMBER OF MANGOS SOLD 1,500	

1. Calculate how many more mangos Mr. Mackey would have to sell on Tuesday to bring the total sales for the five days to 1,500 mangos.

   Answer: _____ [3]

2. There are 8,050 words in a reading book. If each page in the book contains 50 words, how many pages does the book have?

   Answer: _____ [2]

3. BAMSI collected 480 watermelons. After selling 1/6 of the stock, 3/8 of the remaining watermelons spoiled. How many of the watermelons in the remaining stock could still be sold?

Answer: _____ [3]

4. Chloe is taller Tasha. Tasha is taller than Tristan. Kelsi is shorter than Tristan. Tristan is shorter than Chloe and Lily is the tallest of the group.

   Arrange the names of each person in the group from shortest to tallest.

Answer: [2]

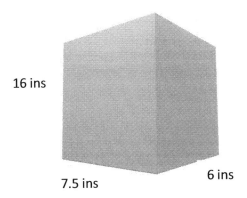

5. Danny's toolbox has a height of 16 inches, a width of 7.5 inches. And a length of 6 ins. What is the volume of the toolbox?

Answer: _____ [2]

Use the diagram to answer question 6.

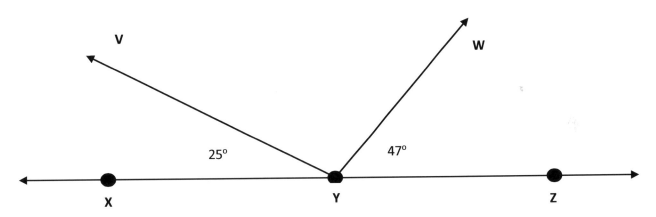

6. Calculate the measure of angle $\overline{VYW}$.

Answer: _____ [2]

Use the diagram to answer questions 7 (a) and 7 (b).

```
                The Mackey's Living Room
20 ft.    12 ft.
                      FLOOR MAT

                         20 ft.

                         28 ft.
```

7. (a) Find the area of the floor mat.

   Answer: _____ [2]

7. (b) Find the area of the entire floor.

   Answer: _____ [2]

7. (c) Find the area of the surface that is **NOT** covered by the floor mat.

   Answer: _____ [2]

ITEMS ON SPECIAL	
28 Oz. Orange Juice	$3.99
1 Gallon Milk	$4.59
1 Loaf of Bread	$2.99
1 Block of Cheese	$3.39

8. Lana bought one gallon of milk, two loaves of bread, a block of cheese and four bottles of juice.

   (a) What was the total amount of money that Lana paid for the items?

   Answer: _____ [3]

   (b) When Lana paid for her groceries, she received $4.81 change. How much money did she give the cashier?

   Answer: _____ [2]

Use the chart to answer questions 9 (a) & 9 (b).

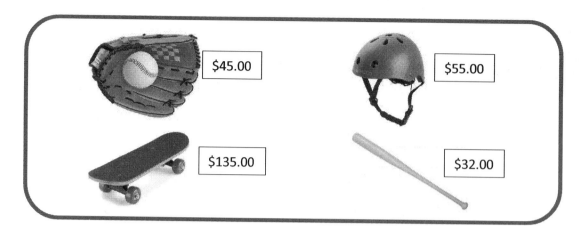

9. The Sporting Centre is having a 20% storewide sale. Kyle wants to purchase a skateboard and a helmet.

   (a) Find the sale price of the items after the discount is applied.

   Answer: _____[3]

   (b) Calculate Kyle's total savings.

   Answer: _____[1]

10. (a) The Bahamas Fast Ferries left Potter's Cay dock to travel to Harbour Island. The travel time was 2 hours and 45 minutes. The boat arrived on Harbour Island at 10:30 a.m. At what time did the Bahamas Fast Ferries leave Potter's Cay Dock?

Answer: _____ [3]

10. (b) Express your answer from 10(a) above in 24 hour time interval.

Answer: _____ [1]

Use the data from the chart to answer questions 11 (a), 11 (b) and 11 (c).

New Providence Western District Primary Schools	
NAME OF SCHOOL	STUDENT POPULATION
Claridge Primary	750 students
Uriah McPhee	250 students
Thelma Gibson	900 students
Sadie Curtis	700 students
Sandilands Primary	800 students

11. (a) Find the range of the data that is shown on the chart.

Answer: _____ [2]

11. (b) Calculate the total population of primary school students from the Western District of New Providence that is shown on the chart.

Answer: _____ [2]

11. (c) Plot the data from the chart on the graph below. Correctly join the points to construct a completed line graph.

Answer: [3]

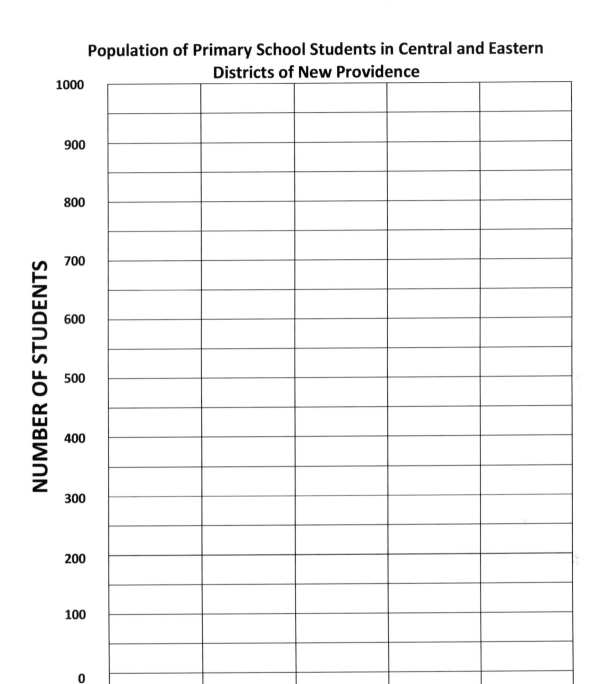

For Answer Key Go To:

http://greatminds.teachable.com/courses/glat-workbook-answer-keys/

APPLICATION - MAY 2019

1. Crystal travelled a distance of 710 km. Kate travelled a distance of 629 km.

    (a) Calculate the total distance that both girls travelled.

    Answer=_____[1]

    (b) How many more kilometers did Crystal travel than Kate?

    Answer=_____[2]

2. Atlantis Royal Towers has twenty-four floors. Each floor can house 257 guests. What is the total number of guests that can occupy the hotel at the same time?

    Answer=_____[2]

3. Esso gas station is giving away 3 780 gallons of gas to its first 36 customers. If the gas is distributed in equal portions, how many gallons of gas will each customer receive?

Answer=_____[2]

	MRS. THOMPSON'S CHECKBOOK RECORD FOR JULY			
CHECK #	DATE	DESCRIPTION	AMOUNT	BALANCE
00	05.07.2018	Balance brought forward		$712.06
53	05.07.2018	Gas for car	$30.00	(a) ?
54	07.07.2018	Spa treatment	$99.99	$582.07
55	10.07.2018	Deposit	$175.85	(b)

4. Fill in the amounts for sections (a) and (b) on Mrs. Thompson record sheet to complete it. Write your answers on the lines below.

Answer (a)_____[2]

Answer (b)_____[2]

Use the chart to answer question 5.

BAHAMAS TELECOMMUNICATIONS COMPANY LTD	
CALLING LIST	
First three minutes	= $0.50
Each additional minute	= $0.10

5. Joyce paid #3.50 for a phone call. How long was Joyce's call?

   Answer:_____[3]

6. Jerry works for a newspaper company. He was allowed to keep 15% of the money that he collected from his sales. In one week he collected $60.00 from his sales.

   (a) How much money would Jerry keep from his sales?

   Answer:_____[2]

   (b) How much money would Jerry give to his boss?

   Answer:_____[2]

7. There are 1029 grade six students in Sybil Strachan Primary School. $\frac{4}{7}$ of the students are girls and the remainder are boys.

(a) What is the total number of girls at the school?

Answer:_____[2]

(b) What is the possibility of choosing a girl from the group of students?

Answer:_____[1]

(c) Find the ratio of girls to boys in the school.

Answer:_____[2]

Use the triangle to answer questions 8(a) and 8(b).

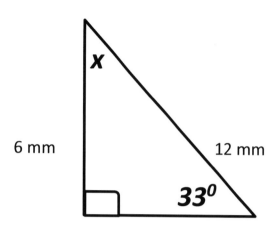

8. (a) Find the area of the triangle.

Answer:_____[2]

(b) Calculate the value of the angle 'X'.

Answer:_____[2]

Use the chart to answer question 9.

BUSES	From Bus Stop 1 to Bus Stop 2	From Bus Stop 2 to Bus Stop 3	From Bus Stop 3 to Bus Stop 4
#15	5 mins. 50 secs	12 mins. 55 secs	6 mins. 43 secs
#21	6 mins. 12 secs	13 mins. 15 secs	8 mins. 59 secs

9. How long does it take bus 15 to travel from bus stop one to bus stop four?

Answer:_____[3]

10. Zion jogged $\frac{3}{7}$ miles on Monday and another $\frac{9}{14}$ miles on Tuesday.

(a) How many miles did Zion jog on the two days combined?

Answer:_____[2]

(b) Zion's goal is to run 10 miles. How many more miles will he have to run to meet his goal?

Answer:_____[2]

Use the graph to answer question 11.(a), 11.(b), 11.(c) and 11.(d).

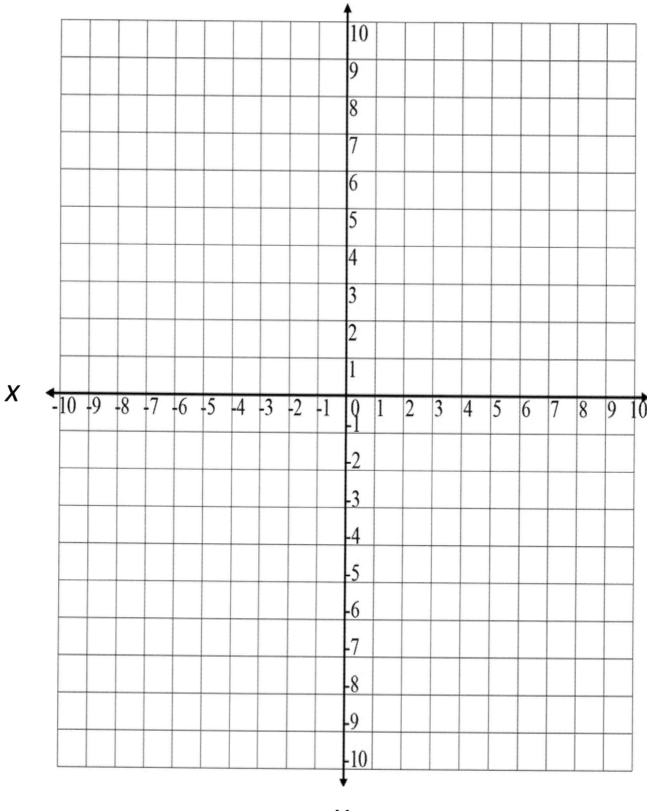

11. (a) Plot and label the points on the graph for the ordered pairs shown below.

        (E)   (-2, +3)
        (F)   (-4, 0)
        (G)   (-4, +6)
        (H)   (-6, +3)

                                                                            Answer: [2]

(b) Correctly join the points on the graph to create a completed shape then name the quadrilateral that was formed.

        Answer:_____[1]

(c) Plot and join the points shown below.

        (E)   (+4, 0)
        (F)   (+2, +3)
        (G)   (+4, +6)
        (H)   (+6, +3)

        Answer:_____[2]

(d) Name the transformation that took place to move quadrilateral EFGH to its new location on the grid.

        Answer:_____[2]

For Answer Key Go To:

http://greatminds.teachable.com/courses/glat-workbook-answer-keys/

REFERENCES

1. Ministry of Education, Examination and Assessment Division, Grade Level Assessment Test – 6, Mathematics May 2011

2. Ministry of Education, Examination and Assessment Division, Grade Level Assessment Test – 6, Mathematics May 2012

3. Ministry of Education, Examination and Assessment Division, Grade Level Assessment Test – 6, Mathematics May 2013

4. Ministry of Education, Examination and Assessment Division, Grade Level Assessment Test – 6, Mathematics May 2014

5. Ministry of Education, Examination and Assessment Division, Grade Level Assessment Test – 6, Mathematics May 2015

6. Ministry of Education, Examination and Assessment Division, Grade Level Assessment Test – 6, Mathematics May 2016

7. Ministry of Education, Examination and Assessment Division, Grade Level Assessment Test – 6, Mathematics May 2017

8. Ministry of Education, Examination and Assessment Division, Grade Level Assessment Test – 6, Mathematics May 2018

9. Ministry of Education, Examination and Assessment Division, Grade Level Assessment Test – 6, Mathematics May 2019

Made in the USA
Columbia, SC
06 February 2023